# THE SUGAR BUSH! CHRONICLES

## ADVENTURES WITH THE WORLD'S MOST PHOTOGRAPHED SQUIRREL

Sugar Bush Squirrel

STERLING
New York

STERLING
New York

An Imprint of Sterling Publishing
1166 Avenue of the Americas
New York, NY 10036

Text © 2015 by Lou Harry
Sugar Bush Photographs © 2015 by Kelly Foxton
Crossword © 2015 by Francis Heaney

A complete list of photo credits appears on page 95.

Interior Design by Philip Buchanan

ISBN 978-1-4549-1466-2

Distributed in Canada by Sterling Publishing
℅ Canadian Manda Group, 165 Dufferin Street
Toronto, Ontario, Canada M6K 3H6
Distributed in the United Kingdom by GMC Distribution Services
Castle Place, 166 High Street, Lewes, East Sussex, England BN7 1XU
Distributed in Australia by Capricorn Link (Australia) Pty. Ltd.
P.O. Box 704, Windsor, NSW 2756, Australia

For information about custom editions, special sales, and premium and
corporate purchases, please contact Sterling Special Sales at 800-805-5489
or specialsales@sterlingpublishing.com.

Manufactured in Canada

2 4 6 8 10 9 7 5 3 1

www.sterlingpublishing.com

# CONTENTS

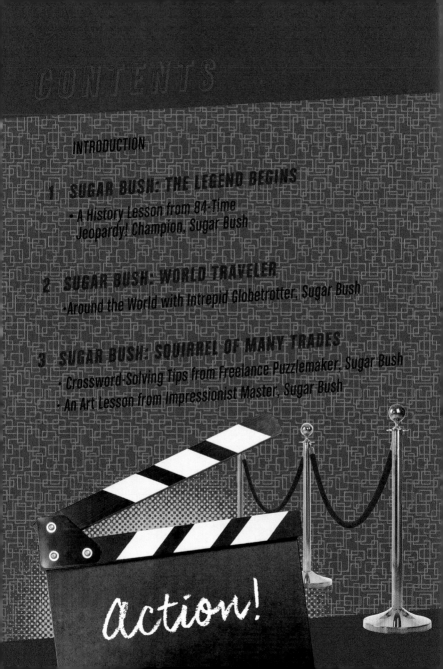

*action!*

Eeeek!

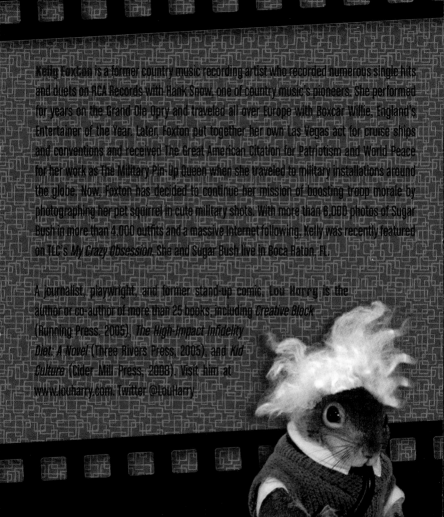

# ABOUT THE AUTHORS

Kelly Foxton is a former country music recording artist who recorded numerous single hits and duets on RCA Records with Hank Snow, one of country music's pioneers. She performed for years on the Grand Ole Opry and traveled all over Europe with Boxcar Willie, England's Entertainer of the Year. Later, Foxton put together her own Las Vegas act for cruise ships and conventions and received The Great American Citation for Patriotism and World Peace for her work as The Military Pin-Up Queen when she traveled to military installations around the globe. Now, Foxton has decided to continue her mission of boosting troop morale by photographing her pet squirrel in cute military shots. With more than 6,000 photos of Sugar Bush in more than 4,000 outfits and a massive Internet following, Kelly was recently featured on TLC's *My Crazy Obsession*. She and Sugar Bush live in Boca Raton, FL.

A journalist, playwright, and former stand-up comic, Lou Harry is the author or co-author of more than 25 books, including *Creative Block* (Running Press, 2005), *The High-Impact Infidelity Diet: A Novel* (Three Rivers Press, 2005), and *Kid Culture* (Cider Mill Press, 2008). Visit him at www.louharry.com. Twitter @LouHarry.

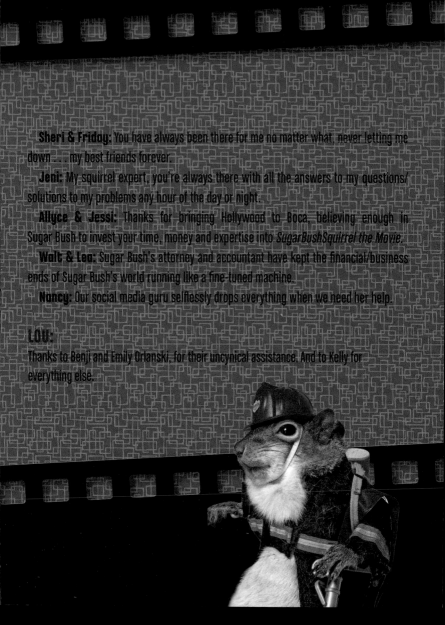

**Sheri & Friday:** You have always been there for me no matter what, never letting me down . . . my best friends forever.

**Jeni:** My squirrel expert, you're always there with all the answers to my questions/solutions to my problems any hour of the day or night.

**Allyce & Jessi:** Thanks for bringing Hollywood to Boca, believing enough in Sugar Bush to invest your time, money and expertise into *SugarBushSquirrel the Movie*.

**Walt & Leo:** Sugar Bush's attorney and accountant have kept the financial/business ends of Sugar Bush's world running like a fine-tuned machine.

**Nancy:** Our social media guru selflessly drops everything when we need her help.

## LOU:

Thanks to Benji and Emily Orlanski, for their uncynical assistance. And to Kelly for everything else.

# ACKNOWLEDGMENTS

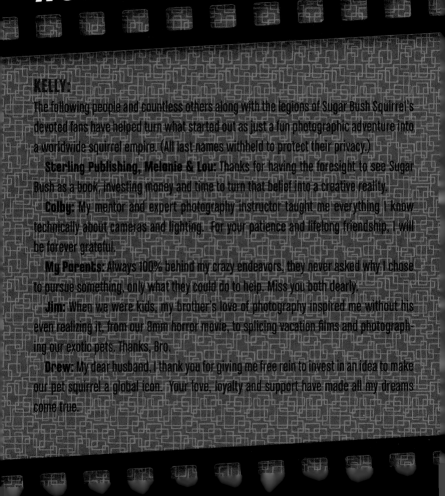

## KELLY:

The following people and countless others along with the legions of Sugar Bush Squirrel's devoted fans have helped turn what started out as just a fun photographic adventure into a worldwide squirrel empire. (All last names withheld to protect their privacy.)

**Sterling Publishing, Melonie & Lou:** Thanks for having the foresight to see Sugar Bush as a book, investing money and time to turn that belief into a creative reality.

**Colby:** My mentor and expert photography instructor taught me everything I know technically about cameras and lighting. For your patience and lifelong friendship, I will be forever grateful.

**My Parents:** Always 100% behind my crazy endeavors, they never asked why I chose to pursue something, only what they could do to help. Miss you both dearly.

**Jim:** When we were kids, my brother's love of photography inspired me without his even realizing it, from our 8mm horror movie, to splicing vacation films and photographing our exotic pets. Thanks, Bro.

**Drew:** My dear husband, I thank you for giving me free rein to invest in an idea to make our pet squirrel a global icon. Your love, loyalty and support have made all my dreams come true.

THAT'S A WRAP!

SADLY, MY REMAKE OF HITCHCOCK's PSYCHO, CALLED NUTCASE, NEVER GOT OFF THE GROUND.

I PLAYED QUEEN ELIZABUSH IN A MACADAMIA AWARD-WINNING BIOPIC.

I kept the costume. It seemed like a good look for me.

Sugar Bush Squirrel

# MUSKRATS OF THE CARIBBEAN:
# THE CURSE OF THE BLACK SQUIRREL

SQUIRREL O'HAIRA IN
GONE WITH THE
WINDOW FEEDER

NUTTY BUMPO IN
LAST OF THE
MOHICKORYNUTS

SOME OF MY FAVORITE ROLES

SNOW WHITE AND THE
SEVEN AFRICAN PYGMY SQUIRRELS

HERE I AM ARRIVING
FOR THE PREMIERE OF
*FURRY POTTER AND THE
SORCERER'S STUMP.*

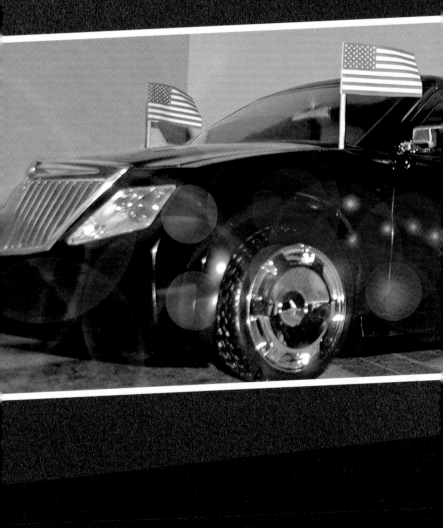

CHAPTER 5

# SUGAR BUSH:
## FILM ICON

**3**

Man, it's hot in the jungle. If you take a nap to refresh yourself, go to 8. If you find somewhere to swim to cool off, go to 2.

You need weapons, so you go undercover to a black market shop. If you buy a machine gun, go to 1. If you buy the Rubik's cube, go to 7.

**4**

**5**

Lookin' goooood. Go to 4.

**6**

You're weighed down by the gun and moving slowly. Hopefully you won't be ambushed. But probably you will be. Go to 8.

**7**

You get so caught up in solving the Rubik's cube that you become distracted. Go to 8.

**8**

Whoops! You are eaten by an owl.

**9**

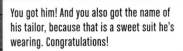

You got him! And you also got the name of his tailor, because that is a sweet suit he's wearing. Congratulations!

# MILITARY ADVENTURES WITH SEASONED VETERAN

## SUGAR BUSH!

Do you have what it takes to complete a dangerous mission behind enemy lines? Probably not, but let's find out anyway!

### START HERE!

Greetings, soldier! Your assignment is to capture a rogue warlord. If you set out into the jungle, go to 3. If you cross an open field instead, go to 8.

**1**

Oof! Machine guns are heavy. If you worked out in the gym, go to 9. If not, go to 6.

**2**

The nearest water is the ocean, so you hitch a ride on an aircraft carrier. If you take the opportunity to sunbathe on the deck, go to 8. If you use the gym to work out until you reach your destination, go to 5. If you commandeer a plane to fly to the desert, go to 4.

THIS AILING AUTOCRAT WANTED ME TO SEIZE POWER IN CUBA, BUT I REFUSED TO PLAY **SECOND FIDEL.**

MY **HOARDING** SKILLS EARNED
ME A MEDAL.

OPERATION MUSKRAT:
BOMBS AWAY!

LESS FUN THAN I THOUGHT.

ANTED

I was assigned to Squirrel Team 6 a.k.a. The Flying Squirrel Battalion.

...WHEN WORD CAME FROM
GEORGE W. BUSHYTAIL
THAT WE WERE GOING TO ROCK!

I WAS HUNTING AWOLS
(ACORNS WITHOUT LEAVES)...

CHAPTER 4
SUGAR BUSH:
SHOCK AND AWWW

Use crushed berries, watercolors, scented markers, washable crayons, or whatever is within your reach to color in the shapes and turn this into a masterpiece.

AN ART LESSON FROM IMPRESSIONIST MASTER,

SUGAR BUSH!

# SUGAR BUSH
## FOR PRESIDENT

2016???

HERE I AM ROASTING NUTS ON *TREETOP CHEF.*

HERE I AM REHEARSING JOHN COLTRANE'S
"ACORNITHOLOGY."

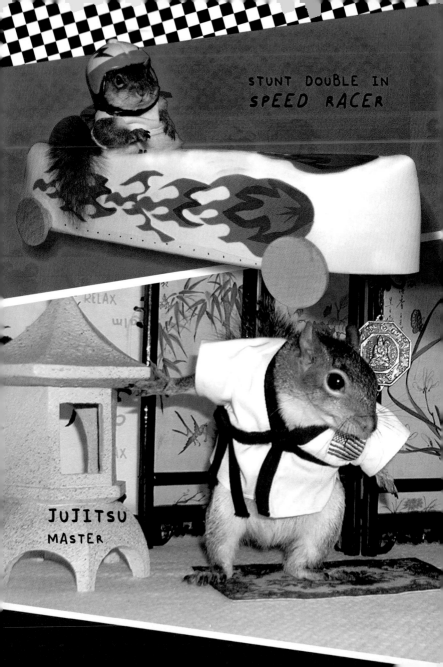

STUNT DOUBLE IN
*SPEED RACER*

JUJITSU
MASTER

GEISHA/"IMPERIAL NANNY"

I VOLUNTEERED AS A "HOSER" FOR
THE BIG BEAVER FIRE DEPARTMENT.

ME AS A MOUNTIE.
PERK: FREE MAPLE SYRUP!

HERE I AM DEALING BLACKJACK AT THE GOLDEN CORN NUGGET CASINO. ACORNS WILD!

MY TIGHTROPE CAREER WAS
ELECTRIFYING.

**7** "How goes it, José?"

**8** One was chasing Richard Kimble in *The Fugitive*

**9** Company that'll hook you up with DSL

**10** Nothing: French again

**11** *The Giving Tree* author Silverstein (I love this book! It's inspired me to take stuff from trees all the time)

**12** 1981 World Series MVP Ron

**13** Exactly right

**14** Without any help

**15** What the Knave of Hearts stole

**19** President or vacuum cleaner

**20** Lamented loudly

**23** Color of tree bark

**26** Aspirin brand

**28** Playground phrase similar to "time out" (also the name of a rock band, in case you're a metal fan)

**36** Classical music work

**37** Yeses: French yet again (I feel so cosmopolitan with all this French!)

**41** Diet soda brand

**42** Soar, like some squirrels (but not me) (unless I'm piloting a plane—which I can totally do)

**43** *Life of Pi* director Ang

# CROSSWORD-SOLVING TIPS FROM FREELANCE PUZZLEMAKER SUGAR BUSH!

In case you're a puzzle novice, here are some tips for you:

1) Sometimes answers are in foreign languages. You may find them easier to solve if you read their clues with an accent.
2) If you don't know an answer, just write in whatever. It's only a puzzle!

**ACROSS**

1 Highest part of the tree
4 *Game of Thrones* network
5 Tic-tac-toe line that's bad news for X
6 What I was when I earned a merit badge in tail-twitching
16 Also: French
17 Dye used to make hair red
18 Vegetarian entree
20 Cheesy instrument in '80s New Wave bands
21 Anti-pollution org.
22 Prize won by Obama
24 Song in the Top 40
25 U.S. swimming medalist Torres
27 Valuable metal
28 Retro-cool sneaker brand
29 Nine-digit ID: Abbr.
30 The ___ Trapp Family Singers
31 Suffix that makes "hero" specifically female
32 "I figured it out!"
33 Sheep that's a she
34 Say yes without speaking
35 My favorite thing to eat when I'm watching the New York Marmots play at the ballpark
38 Sass

39 "What's the ___ of trying?"
40 Streaming service I use to catch up on *Downton Oak Tree*
44 A retail store can't survive without them
45 "I'm outta here!"

**DOWN**

1 Hero with a hammer
2 High-pitched reed instrument
3 "Eight ball in the corner pocket" game
6 Completely full, like me after eating my entire post-hibernation stash

I ALSO WORKED AT A PRISON IN BURNT CORN, ALABAMA, UNTIL I FOUND OUT THIS WAS NOT A **POPCORN MACHINE.**

I GOT A JOB AS
A CONDUCTOR ON A
**MODEL TRAIN.**

(At first I assumed
they would want to
hire me as a model,
but I was wrong.)

Sugar Bush

# HELL's MARMOTS:
# BORN TO BE WILD

So I became a test driver for MaseRATi.

NASA REJECTED MY SPACE SHUTTLE DESIGN. THEY SAID ASTRONAUTS SHOULD BE "INSIDE." WHATEVER!

MY SPACE SHUTTLE

CHAPTER 3

# SUGAR BUSH:
## SQUIRREL OF MANY TRADES

**Ratufa indica**
Location: India

"World's largest squirrel; swank ombre coat."

**Myosciurus pumilio**
Location: Central Africa

"World's tiniest squirrel; can navigate branches upside down, like Spiderman."

**Pteromys momonga**
Location: Japan

Adept flyer; disarmingly cute; "Pikachu of the animal kingdom."

**Sciurius vulgaris**
Location: Europe and Siberia

Varies in color; in Britain, sports a red coat (and sometimes a derby).

# AROUND THE WORLD WITH INTREPID GLOBETROTTER

# SUGAR BUSH!

As you probably know, it's impossible to travel anyplace where you have relatives without them expecting you to drop in for a visit. and I have relatives literally everywhere. Here, let me introduce you to a few of them...

### *Neotamias durangae*
Location: Mexico

Cheeks have impressive nut-storing capacity; enjoys long siestas.

### *Marmota monax*
Location: North America

Aggressive ground dwellers; nicknames include "whistle-pig" and "land beaver"; thinks it can predict the seasons.

THE FALLEN ACORN

IS AS TASTY AS
THE ONE

YOU MUST CLIMB
TO REACH.

I LEARNED THE ART OF HAIKU AT THE MOUNTAIN TEMPLE OF RI-CASHEW-JI.

I FLEW TO AUSTRALIA TO DO SOME **KANGAROO** HUNTING...

After a few bourbons, things got slightly out of hand...
POLICE
POLICE CHIEF
...BUT AS I EXPLAINED TO THE OFFICER, I WAS ON BOURBON STREET!

I CELEBRATED MARDI GRAS IN THE
BIG EASY.

Laissez les bons temps rouler!

IN CONEY ISLAND, I MARCHED IN THE ANNUAL **MERMAID PARADE.**

"The Little Furmaid"

FIDDLER ON THE ROOF: FORGETTABLE

DON'T MISS
PHANTOM OF THE NUTTERY

Give me your tired, your poor, your huddled masses yearning to steal birdseed.

BEWARE: Those ganja cakes they sell on the beach are <u>no joke.</u>

IN JAMAICA, I CAUGHT THE TRAVEL BUG.
OR MAYBE IT WAS JUST A ROACH.

# CHAPTER 2
# SUGAR BUSH: WORLD TRAVELER

PASSPORT

United States
of America

**1979:** **Squirellio Andretti** wins the Indy 500, Daytona 500, and Formula One racing championships.

1793: **Marie Antoinutte** is sent to the guillotine after announcing, "Let them eat corn. I want all the cake."

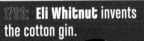

1793: **Eli Whitnut** invents the cotton gin.

1852: The **Wells Furgo** stagecoach service is founded: "When it absolutely, positively has to be there in about a month."

c. 900: Maya worshippers make breadnut offerings to **Quetzsquirrelcoatl.**

1557: **Nutstradamus** predicts the coming of the apocalypse if he doesn't receive "a big basket of sunflower seeds" every day.

1777: **Nutsy Ross** stitches the first toothpick flag of the United States.

A HISTORY LESSON FROM 84-TIME *JEOPARDY!* CHAMPION

SUGAR BUSH!

1333 BC: **King Nutankhamun, (a.k.a. King Nut), begins his** reign over Egypt.

OKAY, SO THAT LAST ONE DIDN'T WORK OUT SO WELL.

I WENT UNDERCOVER FOR A DANGEROUS "STING" OPERATION.

I AUDTIONED FOR THE ROLE OF **SPOCK** BUT MY EARS WEREN'T POINTY ENOUGH.

E=MC² : EATING = MOSTLY CRACKERS. SQUARE ONES. I'M A GENIUS!

I COMPETED ON *JEOPARDY!*
AND MET MY HERO, ALEX TREE-BARK

KNIGHTS FOUGHT
FOR MY PAW.

BEAUTY PAGEANTS POSED NO CHALLENGE FOR ME.
GET IT? "POSED"? I KILL ME.

PREP SCHOOL WENT BY SO QUICKLY!
(PROBABLY BECAUSE I JUST SPRINTED
THROUGH CAMPUS)

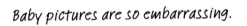

Baby pictures are so embarrassing.

# CHAPTER 1

# SUGAR BUSH:
## THE LEGEND BEGINS

# WELCOME! MY NAME IS

# SUGAR BUSH

You may know me as "The World's Most Photographed Squirrel." As a baby, I was rescued by Ms. Kelly Foxton from a tree that was about to be cut down, and have been living the "good life" in Boca Raton ever since. I've posed for more than 6,000 photos and own over 4,000 outfits with matching hats and accessories.

This book highlights my zany adventures. I've done it all. Or enough of it for a book, anyway, which is more than any of America's Next Top Models.

I hope you enjoy looking at me as much as I do.

Yours,
Sugar Bush

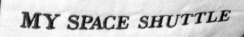

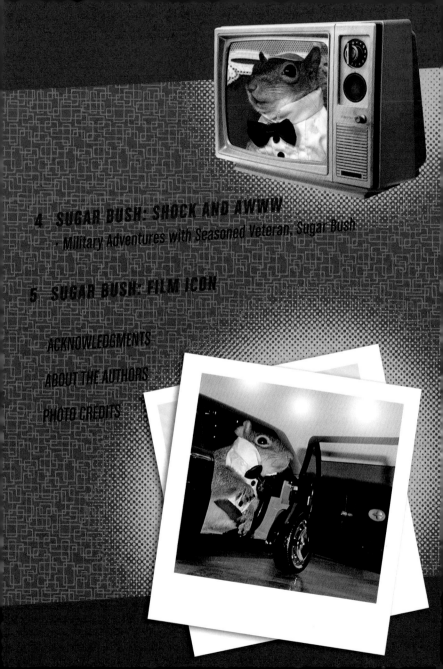